M000239421

THIS JOURNAL BELONGS TO:

........................................................................

........................................................................

A JOURNAL THAT FOLLOWS YOUR NATURE

# Seasons of You

## KAT GRAHAM

Illustrations by Daphna Sebbane

Clarkson Potter/Publishers
New York

When I was a little girl, I dreamt of being wildly successful. My mother fled my father and his abuse when I was four years old. I grew up as the daughter of a struggling single mother who could never quite gain control of her circumstances; no matter how hard she tried, she could never get above water. I needed a career that would solve everything for us. I told my mom that I was going to be a world-renowned actress. I've always needed validation that I was worth respecting. I knew I had a voice and that my life had purpose and meaning.

However, I was met with heartbreak after heartbreak. As a teenager, I tried planning everything—taking hours of classes and training every day, spending my money on music equipment, backup dancing, taking on extra work. You name it, I tried it . . . only to be consistently disappointed, shortchanged, mistreated, and more often than not, rejected. I used every penny I made and every cell in my being to create the perfect life, a better life for myself and my mom. I spent most of my time on this earth trying to gain some control over the circumstances that surrounded me. The idea of continuing a life that was forever out of my control terrified me.

I have always organized every corner of my life. I felt I had to. But then something strange happened—even after tackling my goals, I'd still find myself feeling frustrated, unfulfilled, and dissatisfied. I didn't know how to enjoy the journey when I was so preoccupied with the destination. I was constantly looking ahead, blazing forward, never focusing on the beauty that comes from being present. I was creating actions based on who I thought I was supposed to be, instead of recognizing who I was becoming.

In our lives we go through heartache and loss. Sometimes our lives go up in flames and it is only through the ashes of our former selves that we rise. That's my journey. I've spent my entire life making plans for who I wanted to be and what I wanted my life to look like. And God laughed, so I learned to let go, embrace the challenges, and tackle the hurdles head on. In doing so I learned how to find the balance between planning obsessively and enjoying the journey.

This is the journal that I wish I had growing up, and it is one that will keep me grounded and present as I continue my journey. I wanted to create a journal that focused on wellness, productivity, flexibility, and purpose. I'm the organizer of all organizers. The planner of all planners. Checklists? Bullet points? I've been that girl my whole life.

But sometimes the wind blows that inspiration in your ear, and the snow melts away your fears. And sometimes when you stop and look up, the sun rises at the exact moment that you've been waiting for.

This journal is about taking yourself through the sunshine, the storms, the blooming flowers, and the falling leaves in your life.

These are the seasons of you.

## For Rachel Kim

Rachel, I dedicate this journal to
you. You have helped me crack open
my own seasons and deal with my
own ups and downs through this
process. Without you there is no way
I would've even recognized that we all
go through seasons.

You've been my mentor in this
process and, in moments when I
really didn't want to look within,
my greatest challenger.

Thank you so deeply for being a part
of my journey, my destiny, and by
the grace of God the destiny of many
other people who have needed this
healing like I have.

# THE FOUR SEASONS

You will begin this journal
wherever you are in your journey.

Where are you in your life right now? When you look at the seasons below, are you drawn to any one in particular? Even if you are reading this in the middle of June, you may find yourself in the fall of life, learning how to let things go.

## Winter

This is the season of inner reflection and reset. This is a great season to start with if you are finding yourself in a space where you are ready to take on the next chapter of your life or experiencing a loss of some kind. In this season, we will cover:

• Reflection
• Intention
• Organization

## Spring

This is the season for inviting new relationships and experiences to manifest. If you are ready to bring new adventures and experiences into your life, you are entering your spring. In this season, we will cover:

• Flexibility
• Creativity
• New Beginnings

## Summer

This is the season to radiate and shine through your inner power. If you have recognized your truths and are ready to stand in your power, you have entered into your summer. In this season, we will cover:

• Realization
• Empowerment
• Awakening

## Fall

This is the season for letting go of anything that no longer serves you. If you find yourself in the struggle of change, loss, and letting go, you are in your fall. In this season, we will cover:

• Release
• Surrender
• Radical Change

# Winter

*This is the season of inner reflection
and reset. This is a great season to
start with if you are finding yourself in
a space where you are either ready to
take on the next chapter of your life or
experiencing a loss of some kind.*

REFLECTION

INTENTION

ORGANIZATION

"

My favorite
artist of all time
was Prince.

"

manager was trying to get in contact with me. I didn't think much of it, and actually thought I was being pranked. But a few days later my phone rang. It was Prince. We spoke for hours about everything from music to the spiritual. He loosely invited me to Paisley and then I didn't hear from him for a bit. But eventually Prince called and invited me to Minneapolis to work on some records. "When?" I asked. He responded, "Right now." I had been about to board a plane to Mexico to meet one of my girlfriends for a birthday getaway, but this was a once-in-a-lifetime experience, so I ended up flying to Minneapolis and spending my birthday in the studio with Prince.

From 2013 to 2016, we listened to music, rode bikes, watched films, listened to live jazz, danced, and would be silly to no end. I remember making each other laugh so hard he ran and sat fully clothed in the shower as I was rolling on the ground laughing with tears rolling down my face. I remember leaving one of my wigs at his hotel and him saying it scared him because he thought it was some live animal. More laughter. That was us. He easily became one of my best friends and we never went more than a few days without talking.

One day I was in Los Angeles getting ready to go to a meeting when my friend called me with the news that Prince had passed. My soul was screaming to get out of my own skin. I remember holding on to the dining room table leg as if the wind of the deepest sadness was going to whisk me away. I battled with immeasurable loss, guilt, frustration, visceral anger, then back to guilt. It was almost impossible to heal because everywhere I looked, every song I heard, was his. The world was mourning an icon, but I was mourning one of my friends. One of my closest friends. One of the few people that I felt ever truly understood me.

Losing Prince was the greatest loss of my life. I suffered guilt, anger, frustration, confusion, and waves of depression, but I never allowed myself to sit and reflect. I was so busy living in the moment of the immediate loss that I didn't allow myself to truly reflect on our memories and the words and experiences he gave me. I was sabotaging my relationships, unable to process the simplest things. I needed to heal. I needed to reflect. Reflecting on my memories would mean admitting to myself that he was really gone, and I wasn't ready for that. But I knew it was a necessary part of grieving.

Finally, in a time of inner reflection, I remembered one conversation we'd had. I had picked up his cane and was imitating his walk, goofing off as we usually did, when he turned to me and asked who my favorite artist of all time was.

I looked him in the eye and said, "You, I guess."

He imitated a loud buzzer sound and shouted, "Wrong!" He then said, "You. *You* need to be your favorite artist of all time."

I had struggled with self-worth my whole life. And here I had one of the greatest artists of all time tell me that I needed to be my favorite artist of all time. So I listened. As painful as it was for me to reflect on our time together and accept that he was really, truly gone, it brought back a precious memory that I not only hold dear but also pass on to others.

Now, more than five years later, I meet young girls who tell me that I'm their favorite artist. And because I took the time to reflect and hold on to this precious moment, I can tell them that they're *insert buzzer sound* wrong—that they must be their own favorite artist. As bittersweet as it can be, this is one of the ways that Prince stays alive in my memory. Don't let the loss of someone or something block you from remembering what they taught you. Honor them by using their lessons as a gift.

Think of an uncomfortable experience that you have been holding on to. It could be negative, embarrassing, frustrating, or even something that you need closure around. Write down everything you can remember from that experience.

_____

_____

_____

_____

_____

_____

_____

_____

_____

_____

_____

_____

_____

*Go back and underline every moment within that experience that shifted the way you now move and think.*

Write down why you are different because of it, and what that experience taught you.

_____

_____

_____

_____

_____

_____

Now write down all the good things that might not have happened had that one experience not existed.

_____

_____

_____

_____

_____

_____

Write down how you can help other people who might be going through the same thing.

End your paragraph with "Thank you to my teacher _____" and fill in the blank space with the person or event that caused this experience in your life.

_____

_____

_____

_____

_____

_____

_____

_____

_____

_____

_____

_____

THANK YOU TO MY TEACHER .................................................................

*Reread the paragraph as if you had signed up to be a student to learn this great lesson.*

Do you now understand
why it needed to happen?

# THE LOST CONVERSATION

In this exercise, you will have a conversation with a person or thing connected to an experience of loss. This will be the conversation you never got to have. This could be the same experience you reflected upon in the previous exercise or a different one. Either way, focus on a loss that's on your mind.

For example, if you lost someone and you are struggling with reflecting on that experience, bring their physical being to mind as it was in your life previously. Have a conversation with them. If you lost your home to a fire, visualize sitting in that house as it once was and have a conversation with it.

It will be helpful to have this conversation out loud, so find a place where you can have privacy and space for a meaningful conversation with the person, place, or thing that you need to find closure with.

With the Lost Conversation exercise you are going to verbally walk through the Kübler-Ross five stages of grief, landing, in the end, on forgiveness. If you feel called to journal, write down any insight or downloads you get from this conversation.

_____

_____

_____

_____

*Suggestion: if you want to deepen this exercise, feel free to jump to page 124 for the Ho'oponopono Prayer.*

## 1

Welcome the person or thing that you lost into your space.
Feel free to close your eyes and imagine that person in front
of you, or have the item connected to the experience in your
hands. Whatever helps you get there.

## 2
### DENIAL

Admit to the person or thing the shock and confusion
you felt when you lost them.

## 3
### ANGER

Admit to the person or thing any rage or resentment you
felt when you lost them.

## 4
### BARGAINING

Release any shame, guilt, or insecurity around this loss.

## 5
### DEPRESSION

Remember and acknowledge the sadness
and disappointment you felt around this loss.

## 6
### ACCEPTANCE

Share with the person or thing how you are coping and
adapting to this new reality without them.

## 7

Put your hands over your heart.

## 8

Listen to what the quiet has to say to you.

## 9

Listen to the answers as you get them.

## 10

Arrive in a place of forgiveness, whether you are
giving or receiving it.

Oftentimes a reason why we can't find closure is because we have not allowed ourselves to truly and fully grieve the loss. Closing the reflection is as important as opening and stepping into it.

In this exercise I will ask you to find an object—whether it's a picture, a ring, or anything that represents the person, place, or thing that you focused your reflection on.

If you don't have an object because you are reflecting on a person, take your arms and wrap them around your body as if you are giving yourself a hug. You will hug yourself as if you were hugging them.

Now close your eyes and imagine that person hugging you back. Hold on to yourself as long as it takes to feel their presence holding you. You might find yourself moving in a rocking motion. Allow it.

If you have an object in your hands, place it against your heart for as long as it takes to feel the energy of the person, place, or thing. You might find emotions welling up and may cry as a result. Allow it.

This exercise is designed for you to face your grief no matter what it looks like. Do everything you can to not judge your response to this exercise. You might find yourself in a space of anger, laughter, sadness, and/or guilt. Stay in the space as long as you need to, to bring yourself to the highest states of emotion, so that you may fall apart to fall back together again. This can take one minute or several minutes or longer. Understand the nature of what you are reflecting on and give yourself the amount of time you need.

"

My love for music
started at around
age 13.

"

MY MOM HAD A FULL-TIME JOB and couldn't afford a babysitter so she would drop me off at the Boys & Girls Club after school. One of the volunteers had brought in a set of turntables, and I asked him if he would teach me how to use them. I was so short that I had to stand on an apple box. He introduced me to old-school hip-hop— everything from Wu-Tang to Digable Planets, The Pharcyde, The Roots, you name it. My passion of wanting to be a DJ soon turned into my passion for wanting to make my own beats.

My mom and I were living in a tiny one-bedroom apartment, barely scraping by. I was doing extra work and backup dancing at the time. The money that I made, from my odd jobs in acting and dancing playing posse member number three to being the barely visible dancer in the background, was enough for me to afford my first set of music equipment. In the following years, I began saving up to buy Yamaha keyboards, Pro tools, microphones, drum kits, whatever I could get my hands on. I started making my own music and hoped that a producer would see my spark and produce me, but it never happened, so I had to do it on my own.

I remember years later running around Hollywood one day and meeting Will.i.am from the Black Eyed Peas. I had set the intention that I was going to work with him. After we met, I continued to send him beats all the time, desperate for him to one day work with me. He was the first producer who really took me seriously, invited me to any and all studio sessions he had, regardless of who was in the room. He would listen to everything I produced, offering notes and ideas without judgment or loss of enthusiasm of this scrappy, broke kid with a million ideas.

One night, I was lying sick in bed from food poisoning, having thrown up most of the day, when suddenly the phone rang. It was Will himself asking if I wanted to record the hook to a song called "I Got It from My Mama." I rolled out of bed, feeling like death warmed over, and went to his studio. Nothing was going to stand in my way from working with him. I recorded "I Got It from My Mama," along with another record later on called "The Donque Song" with Snoop Dogg. Shortly after that Will invited me to go on a world tour and perform with him.

This is the power of intention. Had I not set the first intention to work on my music, even without a single hand of support, I never would've made any beats. Those records led to working with Will. I never would've seen the world or heard what turned out to be a hit song played on the radio. It took years from standing on that apple box at the Boys & Girls Club, to buying my own equipment, to meeting Will. I had sheer ambition, unsure of what the future would hold or where this desire would get me. The experience of performing with one of the biggest groups in the world, and working alongside one of the biggest producers of my time, gave me even more inspiration to set intentions. The takeaway here is that my intention to become an artist was long decided by me before the opportunity arrived. Start setting your intentions now, whether the circumstances in your life support it or not. Doing so attracts your dreams into reality.

## INTENTION

Think about your goals for yourself. It could be to gain more financial stability, have a more fulfilling relationship, or start your own business.

Fill out the intention sentences below. The more specific the better. Once complete, go to the mirror. Look into your eyes for a few moments before reading your intentions back to yourself in the mirror. Do this every morning.

*I set the intention to*

_____

_____

_____

_____

_____

_____

_____

_____

_____

_____

_____

# A HELPING HAND EXERCISE

In this exercise you will write a letter using the template below and give it to a close friend. You will explain that you are choosing them to hold you accountable as you set your intentions in motion. By involving your trusted friend, you become closer to your goals by putting them on paper, making them more real.

Dear _____,

On this day of _____, I would like you (name) _____ to hold me accountable for achieving my goals of _____ _____ by the date of _____. In choosing you, I am asking for your support as I navigate my intention of doing _____. There will be moments when I will feel uncertain, defeated, and insecure. I ask that you hold my hand and support me as I move forward toward my ultimate goal. I will lean on you in moments when I truly need support and accountability. I ask that you check on me periodically to help me measure my progress.

Thank you.

Love, _____

# FEAR FACE

*Our deepest fear is not that we are inadequate, our deepest fear is that we are powerful beyond measure.*

—NELSON MANDELA

Oftentimes when we think of our major goals, we don't recognize certain fears hiding in our subconscious that could potentially set us up to fail. Normally, it is not the fear of failure or hardship that holds us back, but rather the fear of not knowing what will happen next and how to move forward when you do reach your goals.

In this exercise, I will ask you to describe your greatest fears of what would happen if you actually accomplish what you are setting out to do in your life. Would realizing your dream job mean leaving your current job? Could achieving a huge personal goal possibly mean changing or ending the relationship you are in? Would fulfilling your intentions potentially mean moving to a new city or town?

Instead of allowing your fears to live in the subconscious parts of your mind, fully recognize and face where you could potentially self-sabotage yourself, and you will gain awareness of what could potentially hold you back. Putting these fears down on paper will help you see how small or large they might be. It will help you address them and help you recognize your own limits so you can overcome them.

Search yourself and honestly answer the below.

*If I accomplished what I set out to do, I am scared of*

_____

*If I become who I dream of becoming, I am worried about losing*

_____

*If I get where I dream of getting to, I worry that I will have to sacrifice*

_____

"

When I was 14 years old my mother and I moved into a one-bedroom apartment in Hollywood—not the glamorous Hollywood you might be thinking of, but the darker, lesser-known underbelly.

"

THERE WERE HOMELESS PEOPLE sleeping under the stairs. There were sex workers on the corner, and our entire floor smelled like a mix of weed and meth. We couldn't walk the dog past a certain hour because it wasn't safe. The apartment itself had a strange moldy smell, and there were always some loud screaming neighbors keeping us up. I remember feeling really embarrassed not only by where we were living but also for not having my own room. I didn't feel comfortable inviting my friends to my home, so I began to self-isolate.

I started dreaming vividly of a better life. I would create mood boards of anything I could dream of: large Spanish-style homes, cars, award ceremonies, red carpets, humanitarian missions, and travels around the world. I tried to imagine (and my imagination was truly my only point of reference) what my life would look like—anything I could do to find a way forward. I would wait for neighbors to throw out their old magazines so I could sift through them in the trash and rip out any imagery that reflected a better life. At that time, I was all over the place—from auditioning for everything as a dancer and an actress to trying to get a record deal and selling my music. I wasn't just passionate about my craft. I was also feeling desperate to get out. But being passionate and desperate wasn't enough. In fact, because of my desperation to succeed, I was spreading myself thin and became wildly disorganized. It soon became clear that I needed to focus on creating a clear plan or else I was doomed to be desperate forever.

I needed to make sure my dreams were the goal and not a distraction. I had to get my visions for myself organized in a way that the universe and I could understand them. I wrote out my yearly goals, my monthly goals, my five-year and my ten-year goals. I broke down each visual I had with a strategy. I did visualization exercises, truly feeling that everything that I was detailing was happening in real time. Writing things down put a different power to my vision for myself. It was important that they become my life commitments. Once I did that, and followed it, my life started to shift rapidly. Oftentimes, it's not enough to dream big. You have to understand your dreams inside out, every which way around, and know what it will honestly take to reach them.

ORGANIZATION

In this exercise, visualize your ideal goal with great detail. Feel free to record the prompts below on your phone and play them back while in meditation.

Close your eyes.

Now place yourself in the exact environment of your ultimate goal.

Are you inside or outside?

Are there any smells or sounds around you?

Are there people around you? If so, who? Study their faces.

What is the lighting like where you are?

What are you wearing?

Are you walking, standing, or sitting?

Now go about this environment as if you already possess what you desire.

If you are around anyone specific, have the actual conversation you would have if you already possessed what you want.

If you are alone, walk through the environment, studying everything around you. Is there art on the walls? Are there leaves on the trees? Examine your surroundings as specifically as possible.

*Spend at least five minutes a day working on this visualization.*

# THE EFFECTIVE MOOD BOARD

Use these pages to draw an image of something you truly desire to become a reality. Let yourself visualize it. Regardless of how large or far off it may seem, commit freely to the full image of it.

Why is this goal significant to you and why is achieving it important?

_____

_____

_____

_____

_____

_____

_____

_____

_____

_____

_____

_____

_____

_____

_____

_____

_____

_____

What is your ideal date for your goal to manifest?

_____/_____/_____

Based on your ideal date, what are the first three tangible things you can do right now to move closer to your goal?

1. ....................................................................................................................

2. ....................................................................................................................

3. ....................................................................................................................

Create dates to check back in with yourself. Hold yourself accountable.

_____/_____/_____     _____

_____/_____/_____     _____

_____/_____/_____     _____

_____/_____/_____     _____

Feel free to repeat this exercise when creating new goals.

# THE TIMELINE

In this exercise, you will draw out a timeline for your dream reality. Do what you can to keep your timeline realistic. Consider all resources and any other obligations you have—travel commitments, job responsibilities, schoolwork—while creating this timeline. Check on your progress periodically to make sure you are moving in a forward motion.

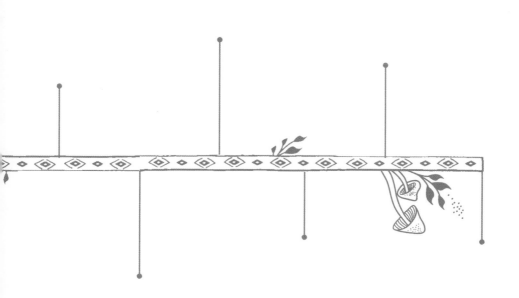

# SEASONAL CHECK-IN

What is your current emotional state?
Are you happy, sad, stressed? Describe
how you're feeling as clearly as possible.
What is contributing to these emotions?

HAPPY    STRESSED    SAD

_____

_____

_____

_____

_____

_____

_____

_____

_____

_____

_____

_____

_____

_____

_____

_____

_____

_____

## ARE YOU WELL RESTED?

NOT SO MUCH ◯ ◯ ◯ ◯ ◯ ◯ YAS!

## HOW IS YOUR DIET?

COULD BE
BETTER ◯ ◯ ◯ ◯ ◯ ◯ GOOD!

## ARE YOU HYDRATED?

UM, NO. ◯ ◯ ◯ ◯ ◯ ◯ 100%

What do you need in this moment?

## Describe where you are in your life journey.

Are you where you want to be? If not, how can you get there? Have you given yourself permission for self-care? How have you been caring for yourself this season? What are some tools you can use to reach your fullest potential within your current state?

Use the following pages to journal about these questions and whatever else comes to mind.

_This is your space to journal_

# Spring

This is the season of inviting new
relationships and experiences to
manifest. If you are ready to bring new
adventures and experiences into your
life, you are entering your spring.

FLEXIBILITY

CREATIVITY

NEW BEGINNINGS

"

It was the worst week of my life. I was 19 years old and had spent my savings from my odd jobs as a backup dancer and struggling actress and had to move back into my mom's apartment.

"

I WOULD TAKE THE PILLOWS OFF MY MOM'S SMALL COUCH and make a bed on the floor every night. She and I were fighting nonstop, and she soon asked me to leave, and at the same time, my acting agency dropped me because they were "getting rid of their ethnicities."

My best friend, Frankie, had to buy me one-dollar hamburgers because I couldn't afford food. To make matters even worse, the love of my life, who was speedily gaining fame for his music, dumped me. I was heartbroken and had nowhere to go. I slept on his sister's couch, only to wake up one day and find that my car had been repossessed. I was broke and broken. I had never felt more hopeless.

I tried to continue with my auditions but struggled with insecurities because I didn't have nice clothes or good hair. Even though Uber and Lyft weren't available then, it wouldn't have mattered because I had no money. Literally no money. My manager had to drive me to auditions or I had to skateboard or rollerblade. Then one night I got a call saying that the producers of a show I had auditioned for wanted to screen-test me. Normally this would excite someone struggling as much as I was, but I had already shot five pilots for television shows that never went anywhere, and I'd screen-tested for countless others. I wasn't going to get my hopes up. I even shot a budget music video with my friends right after that screen test because music was something I still had a bit of hope for. After that first call, I didn't hear anything for a couple weeks. During that time, I enrolled in cooking school since my plan of being a dancing, pop-singing movie star wasn't quite panning out. I looked at my bank account with just 86 cents to my name, and thought maybe trying a new direction and being in a kitchen wouldn't be so bad. Even though I had set out a clear map and plan for myself, nothing was working out. I had to let go of this idea of who I thought I was supposed to be at that moment in time. Then the phone rang. I had made it past the screen test and booked the television show. I was going to Vancouver to shoot the pilot for a show called *The Vampire Diaries*.

Being flexible didn't mean giving up; it meant adjusting to a new path to get to where I was meant to be. The path to success is not usually linear. It takes you on the most unexpected journeys with the most unexpected people. The show got picked up and became an international hit. After sleeping on an inflatable mattress for the first six months of filming, convinced that I wouldn't last on the show and saving every penny I made, I finally surrendered to the universe and bought a bed. Adjusting to a new path led me to playing a non-dancing, non-singing television character that catapulted my career, which eventually led to hit films and hit records. The lesson here? Life doesn't always show up the way you expect it to. In fact, it rarely does. Be open. Be flexible.

FLEXIBILITY

Name three moments in your life that you thought were negative at the
time but that led to a positive outcome.

1. ...............................................................................................................

2. ...............................................................................................................

3. ...............................................................................................................

Name a moment in your life when you underestimated yourself. What
did it feel like? Put yourself in that situation again, but now with your
newfound sense of confidence. How would that experience have changed?

_____

_____

_____

_____

Think of something you are currently struggling with. How are you dealing
with it? What would the situation look like if you do the exact opposite?

_____

_____

_____

_____

Write down ten different ways to reach your one goal. Make sure that with each new version, you are exercising your newfound flexibility.

1. ........................................................................................
2. ........................................................................................
3. ........................................................................................
4. ........................................................................................
5. ........................................................................................
6. ........................................................................................
7. ........................................................................................
8. ........................................................................................
9. ........................................................................................
10. ......................................................................................

Are you placing expectations on tactics that you haven't tried yet? How so?

_____

_____

_____

_____

In this meditation you will find awareness of yourself and the universe that you live in, reminding you of your highest self and your greatest potential.

If it's helpful, record the meditation on your phone, leaving space in between lines to meditate on these words. This way, you can let your own voice guide you in your meditation.

Close your eyes.
Focus on your breathing.

Now, become aware of your legs and the space they take up on your body.

Bring your awareness to your hips, to your stomach, to your shoulders. Think of the space these parts take up in your body.

Bring your attention to your head, your ears, your lips, your mouth, your nose, and your eyes. Think of the space that your body takes up in this room.

Now bring your attention to the room. Become aware of the space this room takes up in your home or wherever you may be.

Bring your attention to the space that you are in. Think of the space you take up in the city you are in.

Think of the city you are in and the space it takes up on the planet.

Now think of the planet and the space it takes up in all the universe.

From the view from space, observe yourself, and who you currently identify as. Find humor in how much you limit yourself to your own identity. Find comfort in your newfound awareness that you are part of this ever-expanding universe connected to an omnipresent consciousness that is limitless.

When you are ready, bring your energy back into your body, aware of the space your body takes up around you.

Bring your awareness to the realization that you are the only you in this space at this moment in time, and you are capable of all things.

Bring your awareness to the realization that you are you in a limitless consciousness that is here to assist you and co-create with you.

Bring your attention back to your breath. When you are ready, open your eyes.

In the space below, write about how that meditation made you feel.

_____

_____

_____

_____

_____

_____

_____

_____

_____

_____

_____

_____

_____

_____

_____

_____

_____

_____

# Flexibility Mantra

"I am open"

Repeat this mantra out loud as much as needed to remind yourself that you are an open vessel, truly flexible, and always capable.

*I am open to all things and the many ways
I can reach my ultimate goal.*

*I am open to the many ways in which the
universe will present itself to me, including the
ways I least expect.*

*I trust the universe to bring me closer to my
ultimate goal, and will remain flexible and open
about the path I will take to get there.*

*I am flexible. I am loving. I am grateful.*

*I believe in divine timing and divine
intervention. I will not second-guess the universe
and the many ways that it may direct me. I will
follow all signs with grace, acknowledgment,
and determination.*

*I am open. I am aware. I will follow.*

*At times, when I feel uncomfortable, I will blaze
forward, knowing that I have the support of the
entire universe conspiring to assist me.*

*I am open.*

"

In 2009, I was finally gaining success as an actress, but my personal life was failing.

"

I HAD MOVED TO GEORGIA TO FILM, but my then fiancé decided to stay in Los Angeles. I've never had much family to begin with, but my mom never visited, and neither did my brother. I was alone in every sense of the word. The life I had back home—the friends, the dancers, the music artists, the LA scene—was carrying on without me. Everything that inspired my creativity was gone. On top of that, my grandmother had become increasingly ill. Because of the filming schedule, I couldn't leave to be with her. The little bit of family I had was cracking and crumbling—and I along with it.

I started to struggle at work. One of the directors pulled me aside and berated me about how I was eating in a scene, saying I was messing up the continuity and calling me a mediocre actress that only got the job because of my looks. I was gutted and felt completely alone. Then my grandmother passed. My mom told me that my grandmother had been watching *The Vampire Diaries* from the hospital bed in her last days and that she was proud of me. I felt crushed with heartbreak that I couldn't be there for my grandmother's final moments, or for my mom.

I traveled to my grandmother's funeral shortly after. In the Jewish religion you take dirt and throw it over the coffin. I remember my brother handing me the shovel and the sound of the dirt hitting her coffin as the rabbi read the prayers in Hebrew. I had to fly back out to set that night since I was filming the next day. The scene I had to film was one where my character's grandmother is dying. I didn't know how I was going to pull it together. I was angry about the way I had been treated on set and that I had to be there instead of grieving with my family. I was feeling so devastatingly alone in a new city with no fiancé, no family, no chance to say goodbye to my grandmother. Everything felt like a volcano ready to erupt.

While prepping for the scene, I picked up a book by the famous acting coach Ivana Chubbuck titled *The Power of the Actor*, in which she tells actors to use the heartbreak in your life for fuel. I broke down the scene to a T, using what I was feeling: my loneliness, the frustrations of my life, not getting to say all the things I wanted to say to my grandmother but never got the chance to. When the camera started rolling, I felt a chill down my spine. My grandmother was there, in all her fierce power. I felt God with me with every line I said. I tapped into an ether I had never tapped into before. My art imitated my life. That moment became my breakthrough as an artist. That place became my home as an artist. That was one of the first times I only had to do one take. I remember the crew being stunned. I don't remember much after that, just my costar Nina holding me as I wept in her arms after they called cut. It became one of my most famous scenes from the show.

I drew creativity out of my own heartbreak, following my need to desperately put it somewhere. Shortly after that scene, I crashed one of Ivana's Christmas parties. I literally climbed over a velvet rope and begged her to work with me, explaining that we were destined to work together. Twelve years, twenty projects, many shared whiskeys, and an Ivana tattoo later, we still work on everything together.

My creativity came only after I lost everything and my back was to the wall. Life does not always deal you the cards you want, but it often deals you the ones you need. I used the cards I was dealt for my own creative growth and expression. May you also find strength in heartbreak.

What is a creative block you're feeling right now?

_____

_____

_____

_____

Is there an experience that may be tied to this block?

_____

_____

_____

_____

How do you feel about that experience? How do you think it changed your approach to creativity?

_____

_____

_____

_____

Use the blank space below as a canvas to express your creativity, whether it's through a poem, song lyrics, or a painting.

Phones are a great tool to keep us connected to our loved ones, to our work obligations, and more. But they also keep us reactive, disconnected from our present space, and vulnerable to being overwhelmed with new information and requests.

For this exercise, you will pick a date to take a break from your phone, your computer, and any other electronics that provide direct access to you. I personally pick Sundays as days to take a break from my phone so I can be present with myself.

This phone fast is twenty-four hours. I would not recommend returning to your phone the same day that you are fasting. The next morning is a great time to do it as some people find their inspiration and creativity after a good night's sleep away from their phones. Give yourself time for your subconscious to work itself out. This exercise is a great way for your creativity to have space to arrive.

Phone fast date is _____/_____/_____

Write down any new realizations you had while taking a break from your phone.

_____

_____

_____

_____

_____

_____

_____

_____

_____

_____

_____

_____

_____

_____

_____

_____

_____

_____

_____

"

As we've seen in
the very pages
leading up to this
one, things change.

"

THIS CHAPTER WAS ORIGINALLY written about my engagement and everything that led up to it. The breakups, the heartbreaks, and the loss that eventually led to a romantic proposal on a beach in Mexico. In that moment, it was a new beginning for me.

But days before this very book was supposed to go to print, I found myself single, unengaged, and flying to South Africa alone for work. There I was, in my *new*, new beginning, still processing the end of a relationship while the rest of my life carried on. I hadn't quite figured out how to talk about it. How could I write about new beginnings when I was only just stepping into one? What guidance could I possibly offer when I'm just newly brave enough to walk forward alone?

I had recently shot a movie called *Collide*. I played a South African woman named Tamira who seeks revenge on the man responsible for her parents' murder during Apartheid. My favorite monologue and the most meaningful moment from the film was when my character speaks about the protea flower:

> "You see this protea . . . they grow all over South Africa. Everywhere you look . . . you know why? Devastating wildfires sweep though there every summer. They wipe out everything, and from the ashes . . . new life, new proteas. The seeds need the intense heat. Sometimes you just have to burn it all the way down before you can start again."

Naturally, the film was on my mind as I was gearing up to visit South Africa to raise money for the UN Refugee Agency. As a child of a white mother and an African father, my relationship with this country has always been complicated. I was coming into a country that would not have celebrated nor welcomed me only thirty years prior, but here I was now, preparing to appear at a sold-out event. It was certainly a good thing. But how could I be so celebrated and yet feel so insecure at the same time, still searching for where I belong?

I was experiencing an uncomfortable transition into a new beginning in real time—a transition filled with insecurity, question marks, uncertainty, frustration, and even more question marks around my personal future.

As I stepped into my hotel room overlooking the South African coast and the vast ocean of the unknown, I looked to my left. There on the table were four protea flowers welcoming me, challenging me, and reminding me that the universe will always offer me (and now us) the signs we need at just the right time.

I could feel the remaining anxieties about my future dissolve. A new peace appeared. There is a particular stillness that comes after the fire, before you venture into a new path from the ash. A new beginning. Your beginning.

You are going to write out two **soul contracts**. This can be a contract with yourself or with someone or something you love or hate. In the first contract, you will reflect on a former relationship with a person, place, or thing that you have not been able to free yourself from.

As you write out this first contract in detail, try to remember to capture the terms of this relationship. You have found yourself in this agreement whether consciously or subconsciously, by allowing certain behaviors to take shape. Take responsibility for the ways in which you contributed to the outcome of this situation, whether it was toxic behavior, hurtful language, or so on.

At the bottom of the page, sign your name.

Next you are going to rip out the page and light it on fire. You can toss it in your fireplace or grab a lighter. Watch the contract burn, burning away that soul agreement that has held you back.

On another page you are going to write out a second contract, a new soul agreement, filled with love, compassion, and understanding for that relationship, committing yourself to your new beginning.

In detail, express the ways in which you are going to show up in that relationship, and the ways you are leaving unhealthy behaviors behind as a commitment to a better future. Sign your name at the bottom; anytime you feel that person or situation returning in a negative way and triggering you, visualize the original soul contract burning and reread your new contract between you and yourself.

# SOUL CONTRACT

no. 1

*Dear* _____,

_____

_____

_____

_____

_____

_____

_____

_____

_____

_____

_____

_____

_____

_____

_____

_____

*Signed,* _____

*Dear* _____ ,

_____

_____

_____

_____

_____

_____

_____

_____

_____

_____

_____

_____

_____

_____

_____

_____

_____

*Signed,* _____

This meditation is meant for you to visualize anything or anyone that you are ready to let go of, allowing yourself to reach your new beginning. In this exercise, you will visualize this person, place, or thing washing away into the sea. It will help you consciously let go so that your subconscious can understand what needs to be done.

*First, close your eyes.*

*Now imagine yourself sitting on the beach.*

*Let yourself hear the seagulls and the waves crashing.*

*Feel the warm sand underneath you.*

*Imagine the waves coming closer and closer to you.*

*Watch as the water washes over the sand.*

Now write the person, place, or thing you are ready to let go of into the sand. If it's a person, write their name. If it's a job, write the company's name. If it's an unwanted feeling that you are carrying with you, write it in the sand.

As the waves begin to approach and take that word away, say goodbye. Place your hand over the word that you wrote in the sand and say goodbye.

Now watch as the waves wash it away, back into the never-ending ocean.

Come back to this exercise whenever you are struggling with an emotion, person, or experience that you are ready to let go of.

How did this visualization make you feel? Write about it below.

_____

_____

_____

_____

_____

_____

_____

_____

_____

_____

_____

_____

_____

_____

_____

_____

# SEASONAL CHECK-IN

What is your current emotional state?
Are you happy, sad, stressed? Describe
how you're feeling as clearly as possible.
What is contributing to these emotions?

HAPPY    STRESSED    SAD

_____

_____

_____

_____

_____

_____

_____

_____

_____

_____

_____

_____

_____

_____

_____

## ARE YOU WELL RESTED?

NOT SO MUCH ⚪ ⚪ ⚪ ⚪ ⚪ ⚪ YAS!

## HOW IS YOUR DIET?

COULD BE
BETTER ⚪ ⚪ ⚪ ⚪ ⚪ ⚪ GOOD!

## ARE YOU HYDRATED?

UM, NO. ⚪ ⚪ ⚪ ⚪ ⚪ ⚪ 100%

What do you need in this moment?

## Describe where you are in your life journey.

Are you where you want to be? If not, how can you get there?
Have you given yourself permission for self-care? How have you
been caring for yourself this season? What are some tools you
can use to reach your fullest potential within your current state?

Use the following pages to journal about these questions
and whatever else comes to mind.

_____

_____

_____

_____

_____

_____

_____

_____

_____

_____

_____

## Summer

*This is the season to radiate and shine through your inner power. If you have recognized your truths and are ready to stand in your power, you have entered into your summer.*

REALIZATION

EMPOWERMENT

AWAKENING

"

I've always been someone who, no matter what, tries to stay positive. When I am met with something unpleasant, I do everything in my power to block it out, especially when it comes to my career. I've never wanted to subscribe to jealousy or anger, but then something weird happened.

"

I WALKED INTO A PHARMACY and I saw part of a beauty campaign that I had been offered but couldn't do because of a scheduling problem. One of my biggest dreams is to do a big beauty campaign, but there it was on full display with someone else.

The only reason I couldn't do it was because they had refused to move the shoot by one day. Seeing the campaign triggered frustration, confusion, and insecurities and brought me back to that exact moment when I felt I had been robbed. Staring back at me was a woman with the same skin complexion, smiling and taunting me. A few hours later I found out another girl had been offered a campaign from the same company, even though I had been told that this beauty brand wasn't doing any more campaigns during the period I had asked about. Again, I was triggered. It was gnawing at my ego. My ego was on fire. How could I have worked this hard just for someone else to receive what I thought I had earned?

Then I had a profound realization. Nothing would be brought into my life unless it was meant to be there, unless it was incredibly intentional. I deeply believe in the power of energy and thought. Where intention goes, energy flows. I needed to trust the universe. I realized that every moment of frustration, anger, and even spite that I have felt has always led me to my greatest victories. Like Michael Jordan, who was motivated by his own coach's doubt, I became fueled by what I once feared.

What if the universe wants me to get angry? Anger and discomfort are not always bad things if they are directed the right way. We are just conditioned to see them that way. It's not a bad thing when it helps you tap in to your greatest potential. After years of trying to "stay positive," I realized I never needed to from the beginning. It is in the midst of discomfort and the frustration that I discovered I needed to make a change, to grow. So, I embraced it all. That's when I took my next step closer toward myself and my dreams. The lesson here is to not ignore the things that are brought to your awareness. Challenges are brought to your awareness for you to face and grow from. It may not always be pleasant, but self-realization is always worth discovering in the end.

## REALIZATION

Make a list of everything and everyone that triggers you or makes you uncomfortable.

Next to each one, write down *why* you feel triggered by this. Remember you are triggered by this for a reason. Think about what that reason might be and how it's connected to the obstacles you are facing now.

Now imagine each trigger as a gift. Write about what their presence in your life is teaching you and why it is an opportunity.

Every time you feel triggered by it, return to this page. Realize and acknowledge how this can drive you forward.

*Trigger*

*Why?*

*Trigger*                        *Why?*

_____          _____
                                 _____
                                 _____

_____          _____
                                 _____
                                 _____

_____          _____
                                 _____
                                 _____

_____          _____
                                 _____
                                 _____

_____          _____
                                 _____
                                 _____

This exercise is inspired by the character I played in the movie *Love in the Villa*. If you ever want to see the most type A person having a tough time letting things go, watch me in this film. This used to be me, and this exercise is for anyone who identifies with this.

For this exercise I will ask you to find a mirror, preferably full length.

While looking in the mirror, you will find the physical parts about yourself that you might have insecurities around.

Verbally and out loud, you will celebrate those things. For example, if I had insecurities about my freckles, I would say, "Hi freckles. I know that I don't give you a lot of time to shine, but I just want to tell you how beautiful you are and how proud I am to have you." If I was struggling with my body changing, I would look in the mirror and say, "Wow, I really love my new curves. I really love my body."

It is important to address the physical parts of you that you are insecure about. Carrying these insecurities will weigh you down. They hold an energetic force that could (more likely than not) block your full empowerment. It is not enough to be empowered by the things that we are proud of, but also the things that we are struggling with.

Make your flaws your superpower. Make your originality your superpower. Start giving your body reverence, honoring the things you are capable of doing—even simple things like moving, breathing, having a heartbeat. Explore all the different ways you can be extremely grateful for the body that you are in.

# THE SIGNS

This is a space for you to document all the signs that you receive. The more work you do to create a harmonious relationship with the universe, the more signs you may receive from the universe as it speaks back to you. If there is a symbol, whether it's a flower or a number, or even a song that holds significance for you, please pay attention and make a note of it here. Signs can also come to you in the form of a dream. Pay attention to all the different ways the universe is trying to speak to you.

Date: ____/____/____     Sign: _____

What it means to you: _____

_____

_____

Date: ____/____/____     Sign: _____

What it means to you: _____

_____

_____

Date: ____/____/____     Sign: _____

What it means to you: _____

_____

_____

Date: ____/____/____     Sign: _____

What it means to you: _____
_____
_____

Date: ____/____/____     Sign: _____

What it means to you: _____
_____
_____

Date: ____/____/____     Sign: _____

What it means to you: _____
_____
_____

Date: ____/____/____     Sign: _____

What it means to you: _____
_____
_____

"

When I was a teenager,
I was obsessed with being
a Fanta girl. You know,
those girls who sang
"Wanna Fanta! Don't
you wanna?"

"

BEFORE I EVEN HAD THE AUDITION, I had the Fanta girl I wanted to be as my screensaver. My mom and I were still living in a one-bedroom apartment in the seedy part of Hollywood. When I heard about an audition happening for the Fanta girls, I showed up and there were hundreds of girls auditioning. As a dancer, this role was extremely coveted. I had no money, so I had cut out and designed my own costume. After a couple auditions, I made it to the final few, beating out hundreds of girls.

I was late for the final audition; it was happening while I was still stuck on set as an extra in a music video. I called the casting director while I was on my way, changing ferociously in my mom's car, only for her to tell me not to bother showing up—the office was closing for the day and the job was gone forever.

But I would not take no for an answer. I had nothing to lose at that point. I didn't want to go back to the extra work I had been doing. All of these emotions were too much and I began to fully cry on the phone to the casting director. I remember saying to her, "You don't understand, I'm the next Fanta Girl!!! You'll be making a terrible mistake if you don't wait for me!" She later admitted to being so caught off guard by my passionate plea that she waited for me to show up. I ended up booking the job.

I remember sitting with the Coca-Cola brand executives at a dinner in Brazil, and one of them said, "You know we realized because you were so passionate about the role that we wanted to give it to you. We saw how passionate you were about the brand." They also let me name my own character as well as two other characters. They even had the designer of the Fanta costumes re-create my initial cutout concept that I had auditioned in, the homemade costume from an old hand-me-down leotard that I had made myself.

I would have never gotten that role had I not first had the intention and enough empowerment to fight like hell for it. The lesson here is that you must choose to be empowered. Take action. No one will ever do it for you. True empowerment doesn't ask for permission.

For the next twenty-one days, you will create an **"I am" affirmation.** Write down one affirmation each day that you would like to embody. After you write it, read it back to yourself while looking at your reflection in the mirror.

For example, on day one you might write I AM WORTHY. On day two, you might write I AM GRATEFUL. On day two, in front of the mirror you will read back "I am worthy" and "I am grateful." Continue to do this, adding an affirmation each day, and repeat the phrases every day until the twenty-one days have passed.

1. I AM ....................................................................................................

2. I AM ....................................................................................................

3. I AM ....................................................................................................

4. I AM ....................................................................................................

5. I AM ....................................................................................................

6. I AM ....................................................................................................

7. I AM ....................................................................................................

8. I AM ....................................................................................................

9. I AM......................................................................................................................

10. I AM....................................................................................................................

11. I AM.....................................................................................................................

12. I AM....................................................................................................................

13. I AM....................................................................................................................

14. I AM....................................................................................................................

15. I AM....................................................................................................................

16. I AM....................................................................................................................

17. I AM....................................................................................................................

18. I AM....................................................................................................................

19. I AM....................................................................................................................

20. I AM....................................................................................................................

21. I AM .....................................................................................................................

For this exercise you will write down a short biography of who you are as if you've *already* accomplished all the things you are setting out to accomplish. This is taking the single line affirmations one step further and expanding your empowerment journey.

For example, if my name was Annemarie and I wanted to have a successful marriage, children, and live on a farm, my "I Is" exercise could look like this:

> *Annemarie is in a successful and happy marriage and has been married twenty-seven years. She has three beautiful children. She and her husband just celebrated their anniversary in Paris and their oldest came to watch the farm. The farm is doing really well, and she recently got a big offer to sell her goat cheese at every Whole Foods in America. Her grandson has just turned ten years old and is healthy and happy.*

If my name was Tom Reynolds and my dream was to own a Fortune 500 company, I would write my "I is" as though I am already in ownership of it, including where I work, who my partners are, what my personal life looks like, how I've accomplished things, and so on.

Write as much as you can with as much detail as you can. Read it often.

For this exercise you will focus on entering the state of irrational gratitude. Irrational gratitude starts rational, with gratitude for current, tangible things in your life. Then you expand and extend beyond where you are to where you want to be, to a point where it is "irrational." I like to focus my energy on irrational gratitude directly after meditation. Sometimes it *is* the meditation.

*Sit somewhere quiet where you will not be disturbed.*

*Close your eyes and find the feeling of gratitude.*
*It might be helpful to think of all the things in your life that you are grateful for.*

*Once you capture that energetic state, stay in it and expand it.*

*Become grateful for things that haven't even happened yet.*

*Extend the gratitude past the now. Expand the gratitude twice its size.*
*And then expand again. And again.*

*Fill your entire aura with absolute gratitude.*

*Irrational gratitude.*

*Kiss the floor, hug yourself, praise the universe.*

*However you celebrate, just celebrate.*

"

I've always been
incredibly competitive.
I've been so used to
losing out on jobs
because of the color of
my skin that I refused
to allow anyone to work
harder than me.

"

WHEN I GOT MY BREAKOUT ROLE ON *THE VAMPIRE DIARIES*, Black girls were rarely (if ever) in a lead role. They were always the best friend or sidekick, and oftentimes, actresses like me were subject to tokenism and marginalization.

Over time, things shifted, and Hollywood woke up and started giving other girls like me a shot.

At that point I was getting older, my twenties were over, and I wasn't being offered the same opportunities that girls younger than me were getting. Instead of being excited, I became bitter and resentful. I would seethe with jealousy anytime I would see a girl performing a role that I knew I would've excelled at if given the opportunity. This was beyond jealousy. This was rage. I kept seeing one girl in particular everywhere I turned, as if the universe was taunting me with her, forcing me to deal with my anger.

My best friend, Firas Frank Elaridi told me about the Ho'oponopono Prayer: "I'm sorry. Please forgive me. I love you. Thank you." I didn't know what would come out of saying it, but I did it repeatedly. And in doing so, I realized that I never forgave myself for not standing up to the racism and disrespect I had encountered in my twenties. I experienced blatant racism behind the scenes, both publicly and privately. I was called the N word, received death threats, and, other than a couple executives, was left feeling unprotected at work.

Where were my flowers back then? Why was I shoved aside and often silenced? I didn't understand my worth back then, but I surely do now, and I realized that the hatred and disrespect I encountered was at the root of my rage and jealousy. I was still angry at myself for not standing up for myself back then. Half of me was unaware of the depths of discrimination and the other half was used to being treated poorly as someone who came from a broken home and expected it.

After I figured out what was happening, I felt awakened. I realized that every actress that looks like me is not competition, but rather an extension of me, and I, her. We are all extensions of each other moving a very powerful narrative forward. I truly woke up from the illusion that I was separate. That connection then extended past people that looked like me and expanded out into the world. I realized that we are all different pieces of consciousness having a conversation with ourselves. I became awakened.

**The Ho'oponopono Prayer** is an ancient Hawaiian mantra for forgiveness and reconciliation. It goes, "I'm sorry. Please forgive me. Thank you. I love you." Repeat this prayer continuously until you receive your awakening.

To become awakened is to become aware. You may be carrying weight that is holding you down. By repeating this mantra and removing judgment you will become awakened to yourself. Start with,

"I'M SORRY."

1. Describe the type of pain or discomfort you are feeling in detail.

_____

2. When did this discomfort first begin?

_____

3. Can you identify a person or event who triggered this discomfort?

_____

4. What was your first thought when you said, "I'm sorry?"

_____

## "PLEASE FORGIVE ME."

1. Describe a time that you extended understanding and grace to another person. What did it look like? How did it feel?

_____

2. Now think about how you might extend forgiveness to yourself. How does that look? How does it feel?

_____

## "THANK YOU."

Write down three things you are grateful for.

_____

_____

_____

## "I LOVE YOU."

How do you show up for yourself?

_____

How do you show up for others?

_____

How can you love those who do not show love to you?

_____

"I am home"

This is a meditation reminding you that as
long as you are you, you are always home.
Many times, we are in uncomfortable
situations or unfamiliar environments.
This exercise is to help you adjust to any
uncomfortable space by reminding yourself
that you are the only space that matters.

It might be helpful to record this meditation into your phone, leaving space in between the lines to breathe through your meditation. This way, you can let your own voice guide you.

*Close your eyes.*
*Place your hands over your heart.*

*Take a deep breath in.*
*Hold it high and bright, breathing all the love*
*and light you can into your heart.*

*Exhale.*

*Take a deep breath in, breathing all the love and light*
*into your being through every cell.*

*Exhale.*

*Breathe in love and light, and as you breathe out,*
*say the words "I am home."*
*Breathe out. "I am home."*

*Breathe in love and light.*
*Breathe out. "I am safe."*

*Breathe in love and light through every cell*
*in your being.*
*Breathe out. "I am home."*

*Breathe in gratitude and happiness.*
*Breathe out.*

*Hear these words:*
*"I am home. I am always home. My peace comes from within,*
*not from what is happening outside of me. I am safe in this*
*space. I feel protected. No matter where I go, I am home."*

To fully trust in the universe is to be fully awakened. This exercise is to help awaken your ultimate potential by taking the universe's hand and saying, "I trust you."

On the following page, you will write the universe a letter. It could begin with "Dear God," "Dear Consciousness," "Dear Jesus," "Dear Nature," or to whoever or whatever you identify the One that you are creating with.

As you write the letter, it is important that you are honest with the universe about your journey and what your struggles with trust might be. If there are signs, this is the letter to ask for them as you go through your journey.

In a lot of ways this is the ultimate surrender. This is your trust fall letter.

*Dear* _____,

*I trust you. I trust that you have my back with . . .*

_____

_____

_____

_____

_____

_____

_____

_____

_____

_____

_____

_____

*Signed,* _____

# SEASONAL CHECK-IN

What is your current emotional state?
Are you happy, sad, stressed? Describe
how you're feeling as clearly as possible.
What is contributing to these emotions?

HAPPY    STRESSED    SAD

## ARE YOU WELL RESTED?

NOT SO MUCH ○ ○ ○ ○ ○ ○ YAS!

## HOW IS YOUR DIET?

COULD BE
BETTER ○ ○ ○ ○ ○ ○ GOOD!

## ARE YOU HYDRATED?

UM, NO. ○ ○ ○ ○ ○ ○ 100%

What do you need in this moment?

# Describe where you are in your life journey.

Are you where you want to be? If not, how can you get there? Have you given yourself permission for self-care? How have you been caring for yourself this season? What are some tools you can use to reach your fullest potential within your current state?

Use the following pages to journal about these questions and whatever else comes to mind.

_____

_____

_____

_____

_____

_____

_____

_____

_____

_____

_____

_____

## Fall

*This is the season of letting go of anything that no longer serves you. If you find yourself in the struggle of change, loss, and letting go, you are in your fall.*

RELEASE

SURRENDER

RADICAL CHANGE

"

As I was gearing up to
write this book, I started
to experience really wild,
vivid dreams.

"

EVERY NIGHT, WITHOUT FAIL, I WOULD ENCOUNTER SOMEBODY FROM MY PAST—a person for whom I still carried an energetic "charge." (An energetic charge is something that is holding your awareness in a negative way.) Each night in my dreams I was greeted by someone I felt had wronged me in some way: an old racist boss who would be kind to me in person but try to sabotage me behind the scenes; or my late brother who had been murdered and who I had never made peace with; or my father who I struggled to let go of, even after his physical and verbal abuse; or former disrespectful and dismissive lovers.

After I would drift off to sleep, they would meet me on the astral plane, and I would have to communicate with them. I would wake up angry, in tears, or just downright confused and frustrated. I had no idea why I was being confronted with people and situations that had no relevance to my present waking life. These were people who had tormented me for years, and I had spent a lot of time and money in meditation and therapy to deal with them, to forgive them. Why was I having these vivid dreams back-to-back? I would try to shake them, brush them off, but they steadied consistently, gripping me by the neck until I had to confront them.

I realized by taking on the journey to write this book that I had to face my past. In order to move forward in my life, I had to release those energies. But to release them, I had to acknowledge their power and existence. I had to make peace, not necessarily with the person, but I had to accept that these encounters left a scar and to forgive myself for allowing them to at the time.

I am scarred by them, and that is okay. I never liked to admit that I had any scars left by anyone. I am an empowered woman, a great artist, a wise friend. How weak would I look if I admitted that these people still had power over me? Once I realized that I had to make peace with what they left me with, my dreams returned to normal.

# THE "DEAR ME" LETTER

This exercise is designed for you to give yourself love and compassion. Oftentimes when we are in a fall season, we stay in grief and are tremendously hard on ourselves. The **"Dear Me" letter** is a great way that you can speak from your higher self, reminding yourself that you did the best you could do.
Tell yourself that you love yourself and that you're proud of how strong you are being in spite of the circumstances.

Remind yourself how far you have come, and all the things you have learned along the way. Give yourself love and compassion and say all the words to yourself that you wished somebody else would say to you. Give yourself some real credit for how well you are doing.

1. Tap into your subconscious and write freely, without judgment.

2. Write down how a tough situation has left you feeling. How has it impacted your choices? How has it made you angry, frustrated, upset, etc.?

3. Your letter to yourself will start with "Dear Me, I'm sorry that I hurt you by . . ." Put yourself back into that challenging situation. Let it flow and do not limit yourself. The subconscious will do most of the writing for you.

4. After you have written the letter, sit for a moment reflecting on the thought that even when we move away from a negative experience, we often find it hard to heal because of the disappointment in ourselves. We find it difficult to forgive ourselves for allowing that person or that moment to happen to begin with. This is your space to allow yourself that grace.

*Dear Me,*

*I'm sorry that I hurt you by . . .*

_____

_____

_____

_____

_____

_____

_____

_____

_____

_____

_____

_____

_____

# THE "DEAR YOU" LETTER:
## CONFRONTING THE CHARGE

An energetic charge is something that is holding your awareness in a negative way. This exercise is designed for you to confront the charge that you are carrying.

Think of a person or thing you're still carrying a charge for. Whether you have just dealt with a death, the end of a relationship, or have been fired, you get to address the person that you are angry with. That person might also be yourself, so feel free to address this letter to you. Write the first thing that comes to your mind.

Write down all of your anger, frustrations, guilt, sadness, and jealousies onto this page. Fully confront whoever this person is that has left you in this state. Hold nothing back.

Let it all out!

*Dear* _____ ,

_____

_____

_____

_____

_____

"

It had been two years since the completion of *The Vampire Diaries* and I was busier than ever. My coach Ivana and I were fielding scripts and offers daily. I was traveling internationally, working with huge beauty brands, being paparazzi'd, you name it. I was putting out this image of myself and it seemed like the world was finally responding to it.

"

EVERYTHING THAT I HAD VISUALIZED as a 15-year-old with big dreams was coming to fruition. I had nice clothes and perfect hair. Everything was highly stylized by a team of expensive and experienced professionals. I felt stronger than ever, and that my path was clear. I was racing toward Oz.

I had five projects come out in one year—more than I ever had in my entire life. I had multiple press tours planned, magazine covers, travel booked for the year, and the list goes on. Everything that I worked so hard for was manifesting. And then Covid hit. Every festival, premiere, and shoot was canceled. I had to get on the next plane out for fear of being locked in a hotel room for months. What now? Movies that were set up for filming after my promo tour got delayed and some were shelved indefinitely. Everything came to a screeching halt, and I was suddenly not making money and back in the vulnerable place that I had worked so hard for so many years to avoid. I didn't want to surrender my fabulous life of hairstylists and fierce fashion. I had worked too damn hard and suffered too long to have it taken away. I deserved to promote my projects and enjoy the fruits of my labor. I spent the majority of my life in clothes out of dollar bins and with bad hair extensions—I wanted my parade!

I went from feeling limitless to feeling blocked and scared at every turn. Scared for my own health and that of humankind. I was rattled, like we all were. My entire world had collapsed in on itself and I felt more lost than found. If the world was ending, was I proud of who I'd become? Was fame, money, and perfect hair the ultimate goal? Did I get lost on my climb to the top? I needed these answers.

So I surrendered. I stopped fighting. If I was going to lose everything I had worked so hard for, so be it. Something was

clearly happening on a profound global scale and I wanted
to stand on the powerful side of it. I wanted to stand with the
universe and God, even if it robbed me of my riches and my
understanding of my future. So I began to meditate more deeply.
I sat in meditation sometimes for hours a day. I gave up this idea
of who I was supposed to be. I took off my wigs and my makeup
and the designer clothes that I thought made me Kat Graham, the
girl who finally got her flowers, and I surrendered to myself, to my
truth, to my soul.

I started gardening, cooking more, and doing everything I could
to find friendship with God and nature. One of the first things
I was asked to do professionally when the pandemic hit was to
film a video for *Vogue*. Normally the old me would've jumped at
the opportunity, but I had shifted in the months of quarantine,
and what mattered the year before simply didn't hold the same
weight. I responded with "I'm going to meditate on it and I will
let you know." I had made a commitment to God during this time
that however long I am alive for, and whatever power is bestowed
on me, I will use it for the greater good. So, in my meditation I
surrendered and listened. I got the download in meditation to
film the video, but to film it with my natural hair. To be honest
with my struggles, and to not be afraid. I'm pretty sure my verbal
reaction to this information was "Really?! You have to be kidding
me." But I surrendered to "the voice."

My hair has always been a struggle for me. My mom would drop
me off at the beauty salon at 9 years old. Just imagine tiny me,
being dropped off by my white mother on Slauson and Crenshaw
in Inglewood and picked up hours later with Shirley Temple curls.
I was never told to embrace myself. I was subconsciously told to
hide it, and that hiding of my hair was further affirmed by every
show and film I did. So you can imagine my horror when God

said to go on the biggest fashion platform in the world and bare my soul. But I surrendered. I did it. The video was a huge success, spawning reaction videos, comments, and millions of views. Women who had never been able to stand in their own power felt liberated because I publicly accepted myself for who I am. This new experience helped me move toward wellness in a more honest and empowering way. I continued the practices that I had already been doing but with a heightened intention. I became more devoted to myself and my practice. I let go of everyone and everything I thought I should be and do, from the movies to the press and so on. I became more successful and connected to my audience during the pandemic, than I ever did eight years on a hit television show.

This meditation will help you achieve peace in the midst of chaos.
To surrender, one must face the ego and liberate from familiarity.

*Close your eyes.*

*Now imagine every moment in your life*
*that took something from you.*

*Think of every person and event that comes to mind*
*that didn't quite go your way.*

*Now imagine that every encounter, good and bad,*
*was sent to you for a divine reason.*

*Sit and breathe through your awareness that you are treasured*
*and there is no mistake in you being here. Sit through that*
*uncomfortable realization.*

*Breathe in your absolute harmony within the universe and*
*breathe out gratitude for exactly where you are.*

*Follow your breath in and out,*
*remembering that your heart will beat and you*
*will breathe whether you are aware of it or not.*

*Surrender to the idea that there is something*
*that is waiting for you, if only you just surrender*
*to the greatness that is guiding you.*

This exercise is designed for you to chip away at the identity that your scars have potentially left you with.

For me personally, as a survivor of abuse, my "I am nots" would be these:

*I am not my abuse.*

*I am not a victim.*

*I am not my father.*

Or another example: If you just got dumped and lost your job, your "I am nots" could be:

*I am not my job.*

*I am not my relationship.*

Observe your feelings as you say these words out loud. Scream if you want to. Refer back to your 21-Day Affirmation Empowerment Exercise (page 112) to remind yourself of everything you choose to be.

I AM NOT ..........................................................................................

I AM NOT ..........................................................................................

I AM NOT ..........................................................................................

I AM NOT ..........................................................................................

I AM NOT ..........................................................................................

I AM NOT ..........................................................................................

I AM NOT ..........................................................................................

I AM NOT ..........................................................................................

I AM NOT ..........................................................................................

I AM NOT ..........................................................................................

I AM NOT ..........................................................................................

I AM NOT ..........................................................................................

I AM NOT ..........................................................................................

"

When my mother
decided to leave my
father in Switzerland,
she left swiftly, in the
middle of the night.

"

FOR YEARS SHE HAD SUFFERED BOTH PHYSICAL AND PSYCHOLOGICAL ABUSE. Between that and the women that he would bring around, it grew to just be too much for her. If she was going to escape that abusive relationship, she knew she had to leave quickly, not giving herself enough time to change her mind as she had a million times before.

She has often said to me that she thought my father was going to kill her. Although part of her still loved him, she knew that if we were going to survive, she had to move, and she had to move fast. She left Geneva for the United States with only me and the clothes on our backs. She said Johnnie Cochran, for whom she had been a paralegal secretary for many years, had to show up at immigration to help get me into the country. She had lost everything about the life she knew, but she was finally free, and we were going to get a real shot at life.

Radical change comes from absolute trust in yourself and only yourself. That no matter what you say or do, or how much you can try to change someone or something, the only person you can truly change is yourself. Oftentimes people don't want to change. Their problems become their identities and they feel lost without them. Even in negativity, there is a comfort in consistency. We allow ourselves to be owned by people, substances, and reoccurring experiences.

Sometimes change is scary; usually it is. But even if you are walking alone, it is always better to grow than to stop. Stopping might mean losing more than you might realize in the moment, or allowing your mind or those influences to talk you out of changing. Radical change begins the minute you understand you must. It happens quickly, not over a long period of time.

The lesson here is that there is never going to be a perfect time to make the biggest change of your life. The most important thing you can do is recognize that you have to make a radical change, then just do it. Chances are you won't be ready.

No one is.

RADICAL CHANGE

Write down one *loss* that you experienced in your life that tore
your life apart.

_____

_____

_____

What opportunities for growth did this loss offer you? How did
you grow from this experience? What did it teach you?

_____

_____

_____

As you write, think about what materialized from your loss.
Do you now feel that the change was necessary for you to grow?

_____

_____

_____

Every time you start to feel the anxiety of change, create your own big win, even if it hasn't happened in the physical realm yet, and write down how important this loss that you're currently feeling is to your ultimate win. It's a great manifestation tool and combines gratitude and awareness. I have learned that even through the loss of my family, I have found some of my greatest wins and life lessons.

---

---

---

---

---

---

---

---

---

---

# The Now Meditation

This is a meditation to bring you into the
now, your most powerful moment in time.
The past and the future do not exist.
Only the now exists.

Feel free to record this on your phone and let your own voice guide you.

*Close your eyes. Focus your
attention on your third eye,
which is the spot in between
your eyebrows a bit below
the middle of your forehead.*

*Breathe in slowly through your nose.
Breathe out through your mouth.*

*Take your arms and reach up as if
you are reaching through the sky.*

*Reach, reach, reach, higher and
higher, and grab all of the energy
from the heavens and bring it into
your heart.*

*Reach your arms back up higher and
higher and higher, grabbing all of
the energy from the heavens and the
universe and putting it back into
your heart.*

*With your hands on top of your
heart you will meditate on these
words: "Today I'm going to be patient
with myself.*

*Today I'm going to be grounded.*

*Today I'm going to focus on putting one
foot in front of the other, not looking too
far ahead but staying in the now.*

*The only moment I have.*

*There is no past. There is no future.
I am breathing love, light, and energy
into my now.*

*My now in this moment is the only
moment that I have.*

*I'm going to give the gift of joy,
bliss, and presence to myself in this
moment that I am living in right now.*

*I am proud of where I am at right now.*

*Reach back up one more time
through the heavens, through the
stars, through all of the magic
in the universe, thanking the
heavens, thanking the omnipresent
consciousness for this moment in
time, thanking yourself.*

*And as you pull your hands back to
your heart, putting all that love and
gratitude back into your being, you
will open your eyes.*

# SEASONAL CHECK-IN

What is your current emotional state?
Are you happy, sad, stressed? Describe
how you're feeling as clearly as possible.
What is contributing to these emotions?

HAPPY    STRESSED    SAD

_____

_____

_____

_____

_____

_____

_____

_____

_____

_____

_____

_____

_____

_____

## ARE YOU WELL RESTED?

NOT SO MUCH ◯ ◯ ◯ ◯ ◯ ◯ YAS!

## HOW IS YOUR DIET?

COULD BE
BETTER ◯ ◯ ◯ ◯ ◯ ◯ GOOD!

## ARE YOU HYDRATED?

UM, NO. ◯ ◯ ◯ ◯ ◯ ◯ 100%

 What do you need in this moment?

# Describe where you are in your life journey.

Are you where you want to be? If not, how can you get there? Have you given yourself permission for self-care? How have you been caring for yourself this season? What are some tools you can use to reach your fullest potential within your current state?

Use the following pages to journal about these questions and whatever else comes to mind.

_____

_____

_____

_____

_____

_____

_____

_____

_____

_____

_____

_____

Below, take a moment to reflect on your healing and growth throughout each season. Which tools will you bring with you as you continue your journey?

*Winter*

_____
_____
_____
_____
_____
_____
_____

*Spring*

_____
_____
_____
_____
_____
_____
_____

Summer

Fall

Copyright © 2023 by Kat Graham

All rights reserved.

Published in the United States by Clarkson Potter/
Publishers, an imprint of the Crown Publishing
Group, a division of Penguin Random House LLC,
New York. clarksonpotter.com

CLARKSON POTTER is a trademark and POTTER
with colophon is a registered trademark of
Penguin Random House LLC.

ISBN 978-0-593-57934-3

Printed in China

Cover pattern courtesy of Shutterstock
© Tile Pattern

Book and cover design by
Danielle Deschenes and Jessie Kaye

10 9 8 7 6 5 4 3 2 1

First Edition